PRESCHOOL B
LEARNING CENTERS

by
Ramona Warren

illustrated by
Veronica Terrill

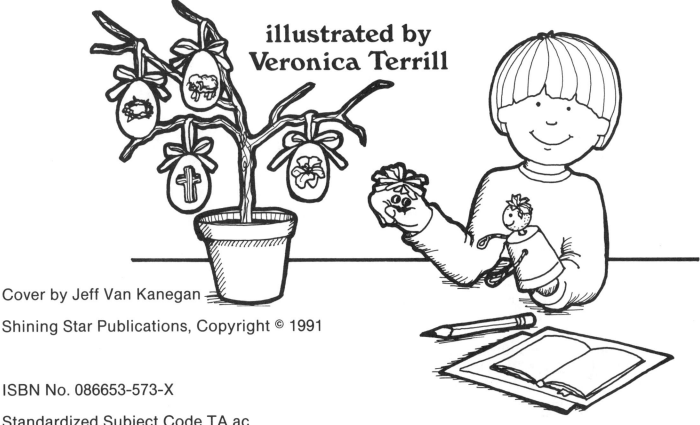

Cover by Jeff Van Kanegan

Shining Star Publications, Copyright © 1991

ISBN No. 086653-573-X

Standardized Subject Code TA ac

Printing No. 98

Shining Star
A Division of Frank Schaffer Publications, Inc.
23740 Hawthorne Boulevard
Torrance, CA 90505-5927

Unless otherwise indicated, the New International Version of the Bible was used in preparing the activities in this book.

DEDICATION

For Jamie, Robby, Becky, Brian, Alex and Angie
who are a constant source of joy and learning to Grandma Mona.

TABLE OF CONTENTS

TO THE TEACHER/PARENT

Learning centers have come to stay in both secular and Christian classrooms because educators and teachers agree they are one of the best ways to teach children. The value of learning centers include:

- Involving the children immediately as they come into the classroom. Rather than free-play which can evolve into a free-for-all while waiting for class to start, children have a place to go to and something to do. For young children this structure represents security and makes for a smooth beginning in the classroom.
- Providing a wide-range of learning experiences as children learn by doing, which includes seeing, hearing, touching, smelling and tasting.
- Promoting social growth as children learn to cooperate and share with one another in their learning center groups. Learning centers give children practice in getting along together.
- Introducing the aim of the lesson through the things the teacher and helpers talk about during learning center time.

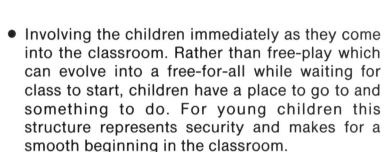

The time the class spends in learning centers depends on the teacher, the help available and the amount of time available to teach. A recommended time is 15 to 20 minutes with larger groups; longer class times may extend to 40 minutes.

Learning centers can be almost anywhere—around a table, sitting in a circle, at a bulletin board or other display area such as a wall or back of the piano, and on the floor.

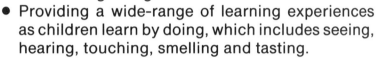

This book gives you ideas for arts and crafts, games, blocks, home living, review, puppets, drama, memory verse music, and storytelling learning center activities, including some seasonal ideas. Use the ideas not only as they are given but as "creativity starters" to build on with your own good ideas.

Have fun!

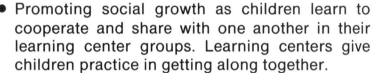

Shining Star Publications, Copyright © 1991 SS897

NATURE MATCHING GAME

"He gives food to every living creature. . . .Give thanks to. . .God." Psalm 136:25a, 26a GNB

MATERIALS:

Apples, oranges, potatoes, grapes, corn, a pumpkin, etc; pictures of fruits and vegetables. (See patterns on following page.)

SUGGESTED SETUP:

Make a copy of the page of fruit and vegetable pictures. Color and cut them apart and place on tables. Place real fruits and vegetables on the table. After the matching game is finished, have an adult cut or slice the fruits and vegetables so that the children may taste them.

PROCEDURE:

- Find the pictures that look like the fruits and vegetables in their natural state.
- Lay the fruits and vegetables on top of their respective pictures.
- Cut and taste the fruits and vegetables.

WHAT CHILDREN CAN LEARN FROM THIS EXPERIENCE:

- how to match
- why fruits and vegetables are good for us
- how God gives us good food to eat
- how to name which one or ones they like best

SS897

SS897

MAKING LEMONADE

"God. . .generously gives us everything for our enjoyment." I Timothy 6:17b GNB

MATERIALS:

Lemons cut in half, pitchers of water, ice cubes, sugar, tablespoon, cups, juicer, picture recipe.

SUGGESTED SETUP:

Place all materials on the table that the children will work on. If the table is not near a sink, provide a dishpan of water and cloths for the children to use for clean up when finished. If your room is carpeted, you may want to place a large piece of plastic under the table to catch spills.

PROCEDURE:

- Put half of the lemon on the juicer and twist it.
- Pour the lemon juice into ½ cup water.
- Add 1 tablespoon of sugar and stir.
- Taste to see if more sugar is needed.
- Add ice and pour into cup.

½ lemon

½ c. water

1 T. sugar

3 ice cubes

WHAT CHILDREN CAN LEARN FROM THIS EXPERIENCE:

- how to follow simple instructions
- how to squeeze fruit for juice
- how to mix ingredients
- how God gives us lemonade

God helps the lemons grow on trees by sending sun and rain. The farmer picks the lemons and sends them to the store. We buy the lemons at the store. One thing we can do with lemons is make lemonade. God gives us good things to enjoy.

Shining Star Publications, Copyright © 1991 SS897

IDENTIFY THE PICTURE

"Children are a gift from the Lord; they are a real blessing."   Psalm 127:3 GNB

MATERIALS:

Pictures of children's clothing cut from magazines and catalogs such as: sweaters, coats, mittens, pajamas, dresses, slacks, shirts, boots, tennis shoes, scarves, swimming suits, shorts, etc.

SUGGESTED SETUP:

Place all the pictures in a large paper bag. Let the children sit in a circle on chairs or on the floor.

PROCEDURE:

- Take turns pulling a picture out of the bag and telling what the picture is of and when it would be worn.
- Or, act out putting on the article of clothing; let other children guess what it is.

WHAT CHILDREN CAN LEARN FROM THIS EXPERIENCE:

- how to identify items of clothing
- how to identify when different items of clothing are worn
- how God makes it possible for families to buy the clothing we need
- how God wants our families to take good care of us because He loves us

     SS897

CHRISTMAS PUZZLES

"Jesus was born in the town of Bethlehem."

Matthew 2:1a GNB

MATERIALS:

Christmas cards that picture the Nativity scene, scissors, cardboard, paste or glue, clear Con-Tact paper (optional), envelopes, a completed puzzle for children to see.

SUGGESTED SETUP:

Place all the materials on the children's worktable. You may wish to cover the table with newspaper for easy clean up of glue or paste.

PROCEDURE:

- Choose a card and glue or paste it to a piece of cardboard.
- Trim off the excess cardboard.
- Cover with clear Con-Tact paper; may need adult assistance.
- Cut the picture into puzzle pieces.
- Put puzzle together.
- Place puzzle pieces into an envelope to take home.

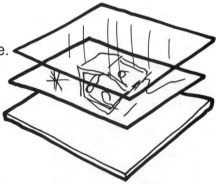

WHAT CHILDREN CAN LEARN FROM THIS EXPERIENCE:

- how to cut and paste
- how to work a puzzle
- that Christmas is a special day
- that Christmas is Jesus' birthday

SS897

CREATION STORY SEQUENCE

"In the beginning God created the heavens and the earth."   Genesis 1:1

MATERIALS:

Creation story sequence pictures (patterns found above and on following page), crayons, cardboard, scissors, glue or paste.

SUGGESTED SETUP:

Make a copy of the Creation story sequence pictures. Color the pictures, cut them apart and glue or paste them to cardboard. Trim off excess cardboard.

PROCEDURE:

● Tell or review the Creation story with the children by laying out the pictures on a table or placing them in a pocket chart in the correct sequence.

EXTENDED ACTIVITIES:

● Let the children take turns putting the pictures in sequence.
● Give each child a picture to tell about and put in sequence.
● Mix up the pictures and let the children put in sequence.
● Use pictures of the Christmas story and the Easter story (patterns on pages 11 and 12) to put in sequence.

WHAT CHILDREN CAN LEARN FROM THIS EXPERIENCE:

● that God created the world and everything in it
● the order in which God created the world

Shining Star Publications, Copyright © 1991   SS897

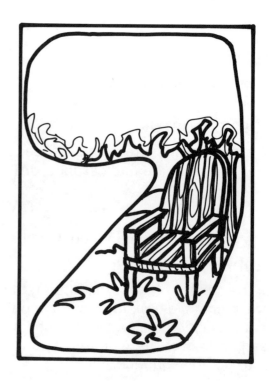

SS897

CHRISTMAS STORY AND EASTER STORY

SEQUENCES:

Use the same setup and procedure for these stories as was used for the Creation story sequence. (See page 9.)

CHRISTMAS STORY SEQUENCE

Luke 2:1-20 The Birth of Jesus

Shining Star Publications, Copyright © 1991 SS897

EASTER STORY SEQUENCE

Luke 22:47-24:12 The Trial, Death and Resurrection of Jesus

Shining Star Publications, Copyright © 1991

SS897

SHOWING GOD'S LOVE ENVELOPE BASKET

"Dear friends, let us love one another, for love comes from God."   I John 4:7

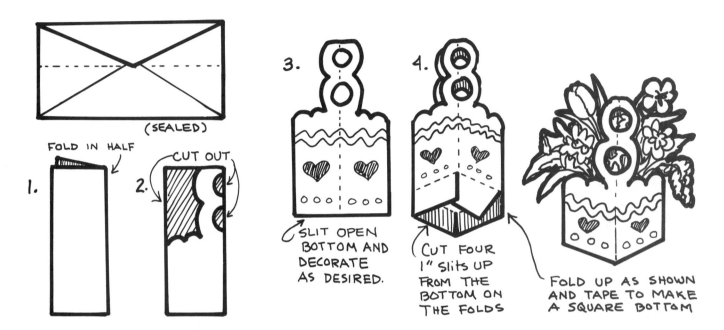

MATERIALS:

Business-size envelopes (glued shut), scissors, crayons, stickers, bits of yarn, sequins, glitter, glue or paste, transparent tape, items to put in finished baskets (see suggestions below), completed basket for children to see.

SUGGESTED SETUP:

Make basket from illustration above to show children. Draw the basket pattern on an envelope for each child. Cover the table with newspaper.

PROCEDURE:

- Show children how to cut out the envelope basket.
- Let children decorate basket while still flat.
- Show children how to form bottom of the basket and tape.
- Fill basket and plan where it will be given.

SUGGESTIONS FOR WHAT TO PUT IN THE BASKETS AND WHAT TO DO WITH THEM:

- flowers or decorated cookies along with printed Scripture portions (from American Bible Society) to give to people in convalescent homes or shut-in church members
- popped popcorn and some information about your church to give to a neighbor or friend

WHAT CHILDREN CAN LEARN FROM THIS EXPERIENCE:

- how to follow a pattern
- how to create designs and decorate with various art materials
- that God wants us to show love to others
- that one way to show love is to make and give someone a gift

PUDDING FINGER PAINT

"God saw all that he had made, and it was very good."

Genesis 1:31a

MATERIALS:

Instant chocolate or vanilla pudding, water, bowl, mixing spoon, finger painting paper or other shiny surface paper, construction paper or mural paper, food coloring to make different colors if using vanilla pudding, water for washing, paper towels.

PROCEDURES:

- Mix instant pudding with water to a spreading consistency.
- If using vanilla pudding, divide and add colors to several portions.
- Give each child a sheet of paper and one or more blobs of pudding on the paper, or have all the children work on a long sheet of mural paper.
- Let children finger paint pictures or a mural of God's creation.
- You might play music such as "The Hallelujah Chorus" or "Joy to the World" as the children paint.

WHAT CHILDREN CAN LEARN FROM THIS EXPERIENCE:

- that God made everything in the world
- to express themselves creatively while listening to music

SS897

MATCHING GOD'S CREATIONS STICKERS

"God made. . .all the creatures. . .and God saw that it was good."   Genesis 1:25

MATERIALS:

Two sets of stickers: birds, animals, flowers; two pieces of 6" x 9" cardboard; letter-size envelope; scissors; tape.

SUGGESTED SETUP:

Place one set of stickers on one of the pieces of cardboard about one and a half inches apart from one another. Tape the envelope to the back of the cardboard. Cut the other piece of cardboard into squares. Place the second set of stickers on the squares—one sticker to each square.

PROCEDURE:

- Place the cardboard with all the stickers and the cardboard squares with the stickers on the table.
- Let children choose a cardboard sticker square, find the matching sticker on the larger board and lay the sticker square on top of it.
- Continue to match the sticker squares to the board until all the stickers have been covered. Store the sticker squares in the envelope on the back of the larger sticker board.

WHAT CHILDREN CAN LEARN FROM THIS EXPERIENCE:

- how to match items
- that God made birds, animals and flowers

You can make three boards and matching squares of all birds, all animals and all flowers or one board with a combination of the three stickers.

SS897

MOTHER'S DAY FLOWER CARD

"Honor your father and your mother."

Exodus 20:12a

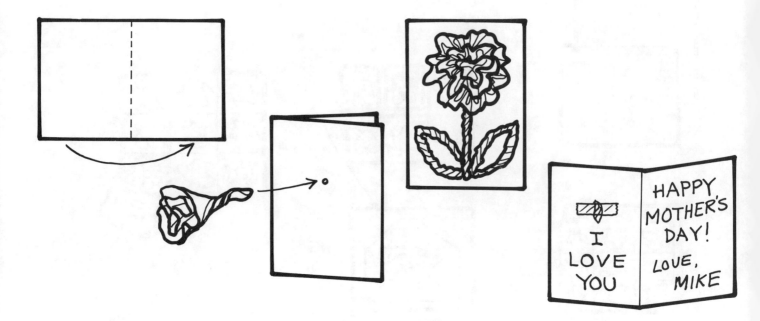

MATERIALS:

Construction paper, colored facial tissues, crayons, tape, green chenille wires, glue, scissors, small bottle of cologne.

SUGGESTED SETUP:

Place all the materials on the table. Print the words *Happy Mother's Day* on a chalkboard or sheet of newsprint.

PROCEDURE:

- Have each child fold a sheet of construction paper in half to make a card.
- Have each child poke a hole in the cover of the card about two inches from the top of the card.
- Give each child a colored facial tissue.
- Show the children how to hold the tissue in the middle and pull about an inch and a half of it through the hole. Tape this piece of the tissue down inside the card.
- Use the chenille wires to form a stem and leaves beneath the tissue flower on the front of the card. Children may color inside the leaves.
- Let children copy the words *Happy Mother's Day* inside the card. Older children may add other words of greeting such as *I love you. Thank you for taking care of me.*
- Have the children sign the card and add a little bit of cologne to the tissue flower.

WHAT CHILDREN CAN LEARN FROM THIS EXPERIENCE:

- how to make homemade greeting cards
- that God wants us to show appreciation for the people who take care of us
- that giving a card to someone on a special day is one way to show love

SS897

BIBLE STORY REVIEW GAME

"He explained to them what was said in all the Scriptures concerning himself."

Luke 24:27b

MATERIALS:

Pictures of Bible stories that you have been teaching the children, beanbag.

SUGGESTED SETUP:

Place all the pictures on the floor. If the floor is tiled, use a small piece of tape to hold each picture in place. If children are five and under, let them sit in a line of chairs several feet away and in front of the pictures.

PROCEDURE:

- Let children take turns throwing the beanbag. When the beanbag lands on a picture, children need to tell one thing about the picture. They may name one of the people in the picture, what is happening in the picture, what will happen next, or tell some part of that particular Bible story.

WHAT CHILDREN CAN LEARN FROM THIS EXPERIENCE:

- how to take turns
- that they can recall facts, names and places about Bible stories

 SS897

NOAH'S ARK BULLETIN BOARD ACTIVITY

Every kind of animal went into the boat with Noah as God had commanded.

Based on Genesis 7:8,9

MATERIALS:

Bulletin board, large wall space or door or back of piano, ark, animals and birds, Noah and family (see following pages), large sheets of blue and brown paper for background, scissors, crayons, stapler.

SUGGESTED SETUP:

Make two copies of the pages of animals. Enlarge the ark pattern. Color and cut out the figures of Noah and family. Cover bulletin board or other large area with the blue paper on the top half and brown paper on the bottom half. Cut open the door on the ark and staple the ark on the background.

PROCEDURE:

- Let the children color the ark with brown crayons.
- Let the children color and cut out the pictures of the animals and birds.
- Give each child two of the same animal or bird.
- As you tell the story of Noah and the ark using Noah and his family figures, have the children take turns marching the animals into the ark on the display. (Be sure to staple the bottom of the ark so that the animals don't fall out!) Then, have a piece of tape on the inside of the door and close it when you tell the part in the story that God closed the door and it could not be opened.
- Add blue paper to the bottom of the board and cover one or two inches of the ark for water.
- At the end of the story, remove the "water," open the door, and let the children remove the animals and tape or staple them outside of the ark with Noah and his family.

WHAT CHILDREN CAN LEARN FROM THIS EXPERIENCE:

- how to cut
- how God saved Noah, his family, and the birds and animals

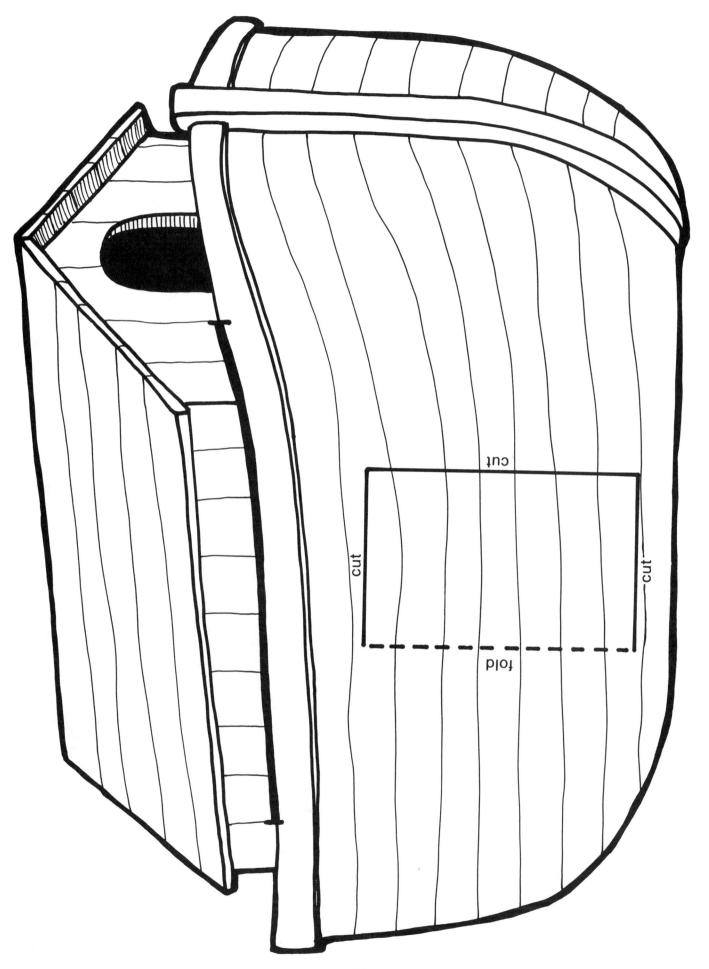

cut

cut

cut

fold

20

SS897

SS897

22

SS897

VISUALIZED BIBLE VERSES

"I have hidden your word in my heart that I might not sin against you."   Psalm 119:11

MATERIALS:

Pocket chart, holder, verse symbols (see following pages), crayons, scissors.

SUGGESTED SETUP:

In advance, make a pocket chart and holder. Make a copy of the page of verse symbols.

PROCEDURE:

- Let the children color and cut out the verse symbols.
- Place the symbols in the pocket chart as you teach the following Bible verses:
  "In the name of our Lord Jesus Christ, always give thanks for everything to God the Father." Based on Colossians 1:3. (Use symbols—Jesus, praying hands, throne.)
  "Every good and perfect gift is from above, coming down from God." Based on James 1:17. (Use symbols—gift package, heaven, clothes and toys.)
  "Let us go to the house of the Lord." Psalm 122:1b. (Use symbols—people, church, throne.)
  "Love the Lord your God." Based on Joshua 22:5. (Use symbols—heart, throne.)

EXTENDED ACTIVITIES:

Play the following review games:
Give each child a symbol to place in the pocket chart as you say the verse together.

- Place the symbols in the chart out of order and have the children put them in the correct order as the verse is recited.
- You might also have the children make a set of symbols to take home to review the Bible verses with their families.

WHAT CHILDREN CAN LEARN FROM THIS EXPERIENCE:

- how to cut
- how to sequence
- how to cooperate in playing a game
- how to memorize and review Bible verses

POCKET CHART

1. Fold pockets along the length of sturdy paper—about fingernail depth.
2. Tape to cardboard.

	1"
fold up	3/4"
fold down	1½"
fold up	3/4"
fold down	1½"
fold up	3/4"
fold down	1½"
fold up	3/4"

9"

12"

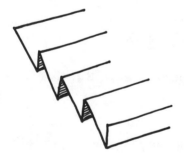

POCKET CHART HOLDER

1. Trace on folded cardboard.
2. Cut out and open.

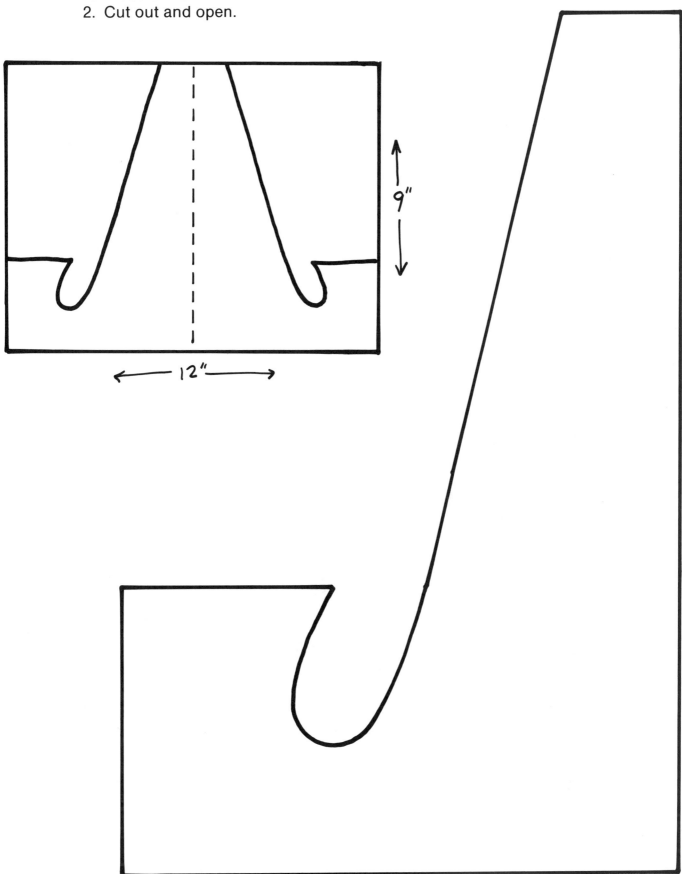

9"

12"

HELPER APRON

"Whatever your hand finds to do, do it with all your might."   Ecclesiastes 9:10a

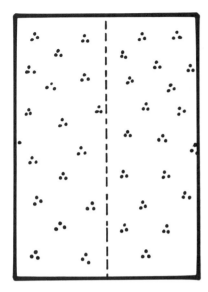 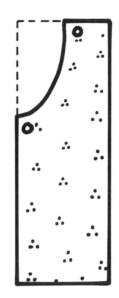 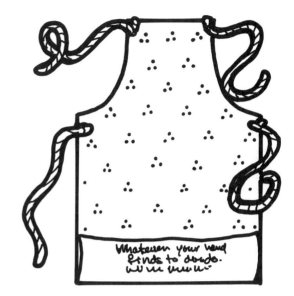

MATERIALS:

Colorful, pretty wrapping paper, brown wrapping paper or wallpaper books, notebook reinforcements, yarn or string, hole puncher, tape, scissors, marking pens, completed apron for children to see.

SUGGESTED SETUP:

Make several folded apron patterns from the illustration for the children to trace.

PROCEDURE:

- Let children choose a sheet of colored or brown wrapping paper.
- Help them fold the paper in half horizontally.
- Guide them in tracing the folded apron pattern on their folded paper.
- Help them punch holes at the top and sides of the apron.
- Help them thread yarn or string through the holes; tie and tape them in place.
- Help them place reinforcements on both sides of the holes.
- Help them fold up the bottom of the apron to make a pocket.
- Help them print the verse at the top of this page on the pocket.

WHAT CHILDREN CAN LEARN FROM THIS EXPERIENCE:

- how to choose
- how to fold
- how to trace
- how to punch and reinforce holes
- how to thread yarn or string through a hole
- for those who are beginning to print, it will give practice in printing
- that God wants us to do our work well

ENVELOPE BOOKMARKS

"Friends always show their love."   Proverbs 17:17a GNB

MATERIALS:

Regular or business-size envelopes, scissors, craft supplies such as glitter, sequins, bits of rickrack, yarn, stickers, etc., glue, crayons or marking pens, completed bookmark for children to see.

SUGGESTED SETUP:

In advance, seal all the envelopes and draw various types of lines across the corners for the children to cut on (see illustration). Cover the table with newspaper.

PROCEDURE:

- Give each child an envelope to cut on the lines to make two bookmarks.
- Let children decorate both sides of the bookmarks.
- Show the children how the bookmarks fit over the edge of the page in a book.

WHAT CHILDREN CAN LEARN FROM THIS EXPERIENCE:

- how to cut
- how to use craft materials
- that God wants us to show our love to friends
- that one way to show love to friends is to give them a gift

                    SS897

JESUS BRACELET

"I will be with you always . . . ." Matthew 28:20b GNB

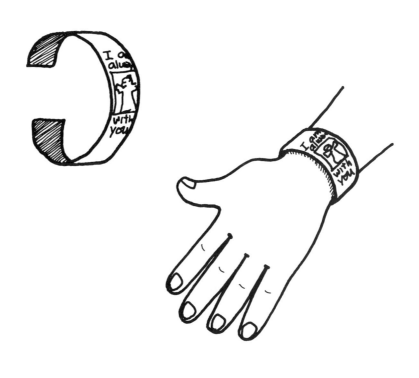

MATERIALS:

Colored construction paper, sticker pictures of Jesus, tape, fine-tip marking pen, completed bracelet for children to see.

SUGGESTED SETUP:

In advance, cut the construction paper into 1" x 4" strips. Print the words *I am always with you* on the strips. As a guide for spacing, place one of the pictures of Jesus on one of the strips and print the words *I am always* above the picture and the words *with you* below the picture (see illustration). Or you may wish to print the child's name in place of the word *you*.

PROCEDURE:

- Give each child a strip of construction paper and a sticker picture of Jesus.
- Help the child place the sticker between the words on the strip of paper.
- Tape the strip of paper on the child's arm to make a bracelet.
- Allow the children to make a second bracelet for a friend or family member.

WHAT CHILDREN CAN LEARN FROM THIS EXPERIENCE:

- how to place a sticker
- be reminded whenever they look at their bracelets that Jesus is always with them

 SS897

WHAT'S IN THE BAG?

"It is more blessed to give than to receive."

Acts 20:35b KJV

MATERIALS:

A drawstring bag or medium-sized paper bag, several items that can be shared, such as a small book, toy, box of crayons, cookie or cracker, Bible, and pictures of things that can be shared (see following page).

SUGGESTED SETUP:

Place all the items and pictures in the bag. Place the bag in the middle of the room. Have the children seated around the bag.

PROCEDURE:

- Let children take turns reaching into the bag and taking out one item.
- Have each child show the item to the other children and tell how it can be shared. Give help where needed.

EXTENDED ACTIVITY:

- Have children remove the items to another place and act out how they would use items to share, as the others try to guess what the items are.

WHAT CHILDREN CAN LEARN FROM THIS EXPERIENCE:

- to think of ways to share with others
- to learn that God wants us to share what we have

To teach the concept of helping, items and pictures of things that children can help with can be put in the bag and the same procedure followed.

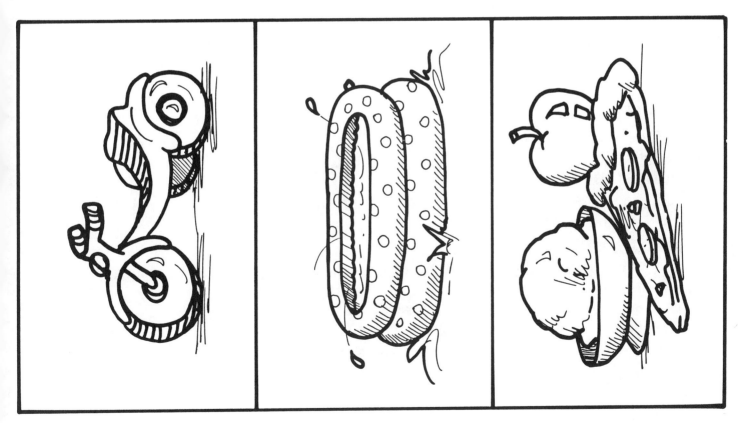

WHAT'S IN THE BAG? PART II

"When I am afraid, I will trust in you."   Psalm 56:3

MATERIALS:

A drawstring bag or medium-sized paper bag, pictures of times when children are afraid (see following page).

SUGGESTED SETUP:

Place all the pictures in the bag. Put the bag in the middle of the room. Have the children seated around the bag.

PROCEDURE:

- Let children take turns reaching into the bag and taking out one of the pictures.
- Have the children show the picture and tell about it.
- Ask children if they have ever had the experience pictured.
- Discuss how they felt and what they did.

WHAT CHILDREN CAN LEARN FROM THIS EXPERIENCE:

- how to describe a picture
- how to discuss a subject
- that God is always with them and they can trust Him to help them when they are afraid

Shining Star Publications, Copyright © 1991   SS897

SS897

BIRD TOUCH 'N FEEL PICTURE

"...God created...every winged bird according to its kind."   Genesis 1:21b

MATERIALS:

Blue construction paper, bird and nest pattern (see following page), twigs, grass or straw, bird seed, feathers, scissors, crayons, glue, tape.

SUGGESTED SETUP:

In advance, make copies of bird and nest picture—one for each child. Cover the table with newspaper.

PROCEDURE:

- Let children color and cut out their birds and nests.
- Give each child a sheet of blue construction paper.
- Let children choose a twig, some grass or straw, bird seed and feathers.
- Help children glue or tape the twig on the construction paper, glue the bird and nest on the twig and the feathers on the bird, and grass or straw and bird seed on the nest. The children might also glue a piece of grass or straw on the bird's beak.
- Help the children print the Bible verse above at the top of their pictures.

WHAT CHILDREN CAN LEARN FROM THIS EXPERIENCE:

- how to create a picture
- that God made the birds

SS897

THANK-YOU PLACE MATS

"Give thanks to the Lord, for he is good."   Psalm 136:1

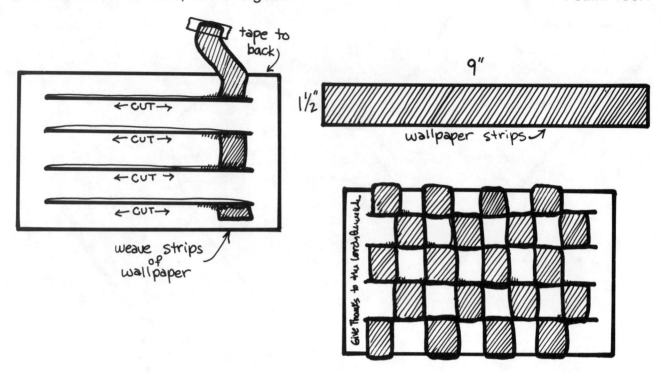

MATERIALS:

Colored construction paper, wallpaper books, scissors, tape, marking pens, one completed place mat for children to see.

SUGGESTED SETUP:

In advance, cut four horizontal lines on several sheets of construction paper, stopping 1" before each edge. Make at least one for each child, more if the children will be making place mats for other family members. Also, cut several strips of wallpaper 1½" wide and 9" long.

PROCEDURE:

- Give each child a sheet of construction paper and four strips of wallpaper.
- Show the children how to weave the strips of wallpaper—one at a time—through the slits on the construction paper.
- Tape the excess wallpaper on each end to the back of the construction paper mat.
- Help children print the Bible verse above on the plain part of the mat.

WHAT CHILDREN CAN LEARN FROM THIS EXPERIENCE:

- how to weave
- that we should thank God before our meals

ALLELUIA BANNER

"He is not here; he has risen!"

Luke 24:6a

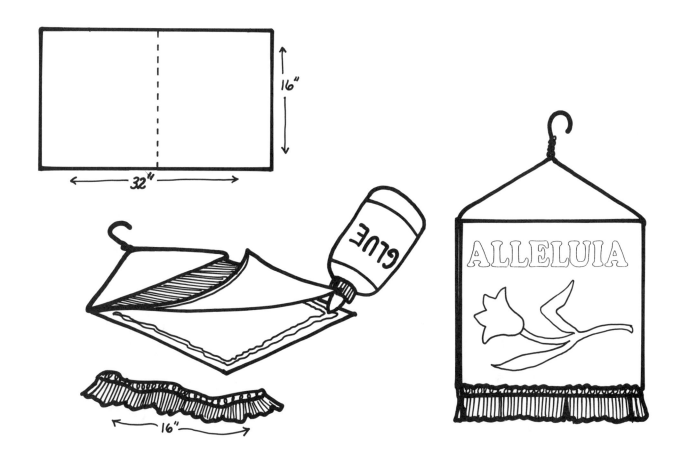

MATERIALS:

Hangers, brightly colored felt or burlap, white felt, letter and lily patterns (see following page), glue, fringe or tassels, scissors, one completed banner for children to see.

SUGGESTED SETUP:

Cut felt or burlap to 16" x 32" pieces and cut 16" lengths of fringe or tassels—one for each child. Also, cut out letters and lilies for each child from white felt.

PROCEDURE:

- Give each child a hanger and piece of 16" x 32" felt or burlap.
- Help children fold the felt or burlap over the coat hanger, so that the bottom edges are even, and glue the sides and bottom together.
- Help children glue on the word *Alleluia*, the lily, and the fringe or tassel.

WHAT CHILDREN CAN LEARN FROM THIS EXPERIENCE:

- how to work with different materials
- that we are happy that Jesus is alive

Shining Star Publications, Copyright © 1991

SS897

ALELUIA

38

FATHER'S DAY BOUTONNIERE

"Children, obey your parents in the Lord, for this is right."   Ephesians 6:1

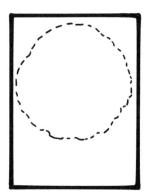 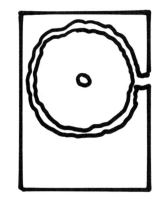 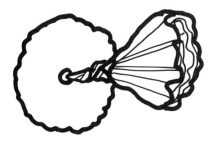 

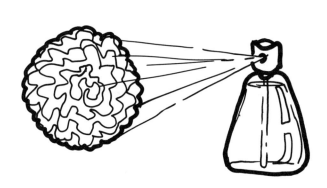 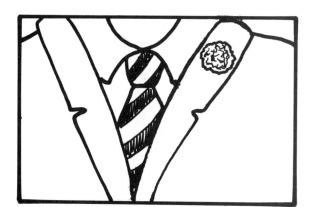

MATERIALS:

Colored construction paper and facial tissue, scissors, tape, perfume in a spray bottle, one completed boutonniere for children to see.

SUGGESTED SETUP:

Have a 5½" x 8½" sheet of construction paper and facial tissue ready for each child.

PROCEDURE:

- Give each child a sheet of construction paper.
- Have the children cut or tear a circle out of the construction paper.
- Have the children poke a hole in the center of the circle.
- Show the children how to pick up the facial tissue in the center, pull it through the hole about two inches and tape the end down.
- Spray the tissue flower with perfume.

WHAT CHILDREN CAN LEARN FROM THIS EXPERIENCE:

- how to make a gift for their fathers to wear
- that God wants us to show our fathers love and making a gift is one way to show love

THANKSGIVING MURAL

"Now, our God, we give you thanks, and praise your glorious name."   I Chronicles 29:13

MATERIALS:

Long mural paper, letters and patterns (see following pages), crayons, magazine pictures (optional).

SUGGESTED SETUP:

Hang the mural paper on the wall low enough for the children to work at. Use the letters to make the title. Cut out the patterns for the children to use as "creativity starters"— children may choose a pattern to place on the mural, trace around, and color. Then, they will begin to make their own drawings. Optional—have pictures of things we are thankful for torn out of magazines for the children to choose and add to the mural, along with the patterns they have traced and their own freehand drawings.

PROCEDURE:

- Encourage children to choose a pattern, trace it on the mural and color.
- Then, encourage children to think of things they are thankful for and draw and color them on the mural.
- Optional—add magazine pictures of things we are thankful for to the mural.

WHAT CHILDREN CAN LEARN FROM THIS EXPERIENCE:

- how to trace
- practice drawing
- to think about, name, and draw some of the many things we can thank God for

OUR GOD, WE GIVE YOU THANKS

VALENTINE CARD

"Love each other as I have loved you."   John 15:12b

MATERIALS:

Raw potatoes, light-colored construction paper, red and pink paint, marking pens or crayons, paint smocks.

SUGGESTED SETUP:

In advance, cut potatoes in half; on the open end of each potato, draw a heart shape. Cut away the potato around the heart shape so that the shape is raised. Put paint in Styrofoam or aluminum plates.

PROCEDURE:

● Give each child a sheet of construction paper to fold in half, making a card.
● Help children print the words *Happy Valentine's Day* on the cover of the card and *I love you* on the inside right page of the card.
● Have children put on paint smocks and roll up sleeves.
● Show children how to dip the heart shape into the paint and press onto the card.
● Let the children make as many heart prints on the cards as they wish—be sure they dip their potatoes in the paint for each print.
● Help children sign their names to the back of their cards.

WHAT CHILDREN CAN LEARN FROM THIS EXPERIENCE:

● how to print paint
● for those who are learning to print, practice in printing
● that God wants us to show our love for one another and that making a card for someone is one way to show love

OUR FAMILIES GO TO CHURCH

"I love the house where you live, O Lord, the place where your glory dwells."   Psalm 26:8

MATERIALS:

Mural paper, church, people and title patterns (see following pages), scissors, crayons, tape.

SUGGESTED SETUP:

Hang mural paper on the wall so that children can work at it. Enlarge the church pattern (see pattern on page 45) and tape to the middle of the mural. Use the letters to make the title of the mural. Make several copies of the people patterns (see page 46).

PROCEDURE:

- Let children use the patterns to make the number of people there are in their families.
- Have the children draw features and clothing on the figures and cut them out.
- Help the children tape the family groups to the mural.
- Let the children color the letters in the title, add trees, bushes, grass, and flowers around the church.

WHAT CHILDREN CAN LEARN FROM THIS EXPERIENCE:

- that many different sizes of families attend church
- that God wants us to attend church regularly

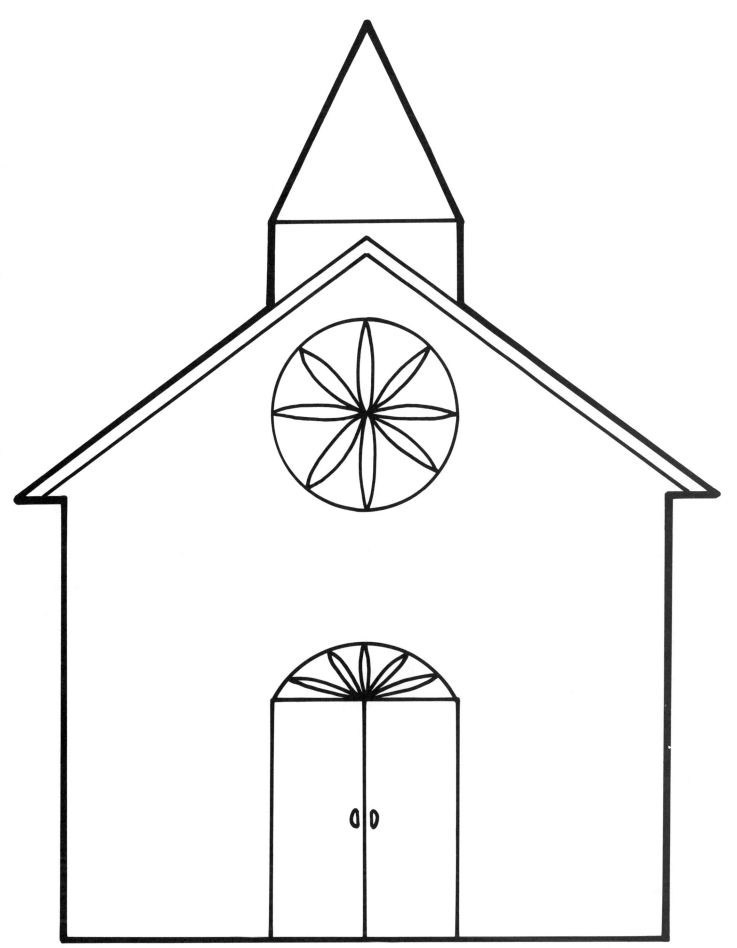

45

SS897

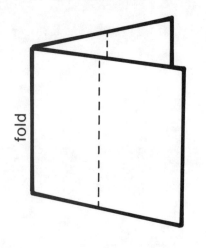 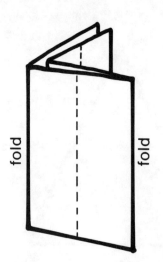 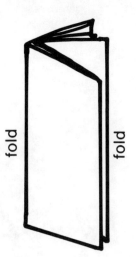 

Boy

Girl

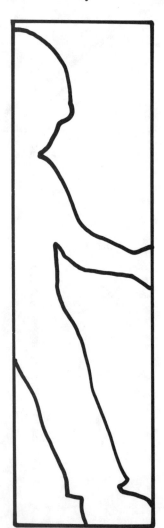  

46

OUR FAMILIES GO TO CHURCH

SS897

GOD, THANK YOU FOR EVERYTHING

"Let everything that has breath praise the Lord."

Psalm 150:6a

MATERIALS:

House frame, child's body parts and clothing, bed, rocking chair with teddy bear sitting in it, fireplace, family figures and letters (see following pages), bulletin board, wall space or back of piano, tape or straight pins.

SUGGESTED SETUP:

Make copies of patterns and letters, color, cut and place patterns on table in front of bulletin board, wall space or back of piano. Pin or tape title to the top of the display.

PROCEDURE:

- Set children in front of bulletin board, wall space or back of piano on which the pattern piece of the child's chest and head has been taped or pinned.
- Give the children each one of the pattern pieces and tell them that you will help them know when to put the piece on the display.
- Read the story and have the children add the pieces as follows:

Thank you, God, for arms to hug those I love.
(Place arms on the child's body.)
Thank you for legs to run and play.
(Add legs to the child's body.)
Thank you for my warm home.
(Add house frame and fireplace.)
Thank you, God, for everything.
Thank you for my eyes, to see your beautiful world.
(Point to eyes on the child.)
Thank you for my ears, to hear voices and laughter.
(Point to ears on the child.)
Thank you for my nose, to smell flowers and food.
(Point to child's nose.)
Thank you, God, for everything.
Thank you, God, for my family.
(Add family group.)

Thank you for clothes to wear,
(Add sweater and knit hat to child's body.)
And a bed to rest my head.
(Add bed to room at top of house frame.)
Thank you, God, for everything.

- The next time through reading the story, have children listen for when to add the pieces and let them do it on their own.

WHAT CHILDREN CAN LEARN FROM THIS EXPERIENCE:

- how to listen carefully
- that God knows everything we need

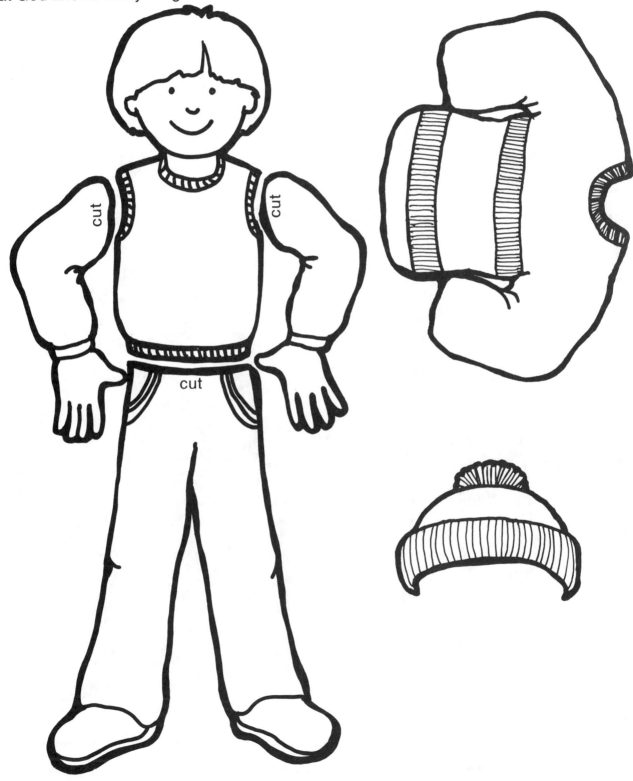

50

SS897

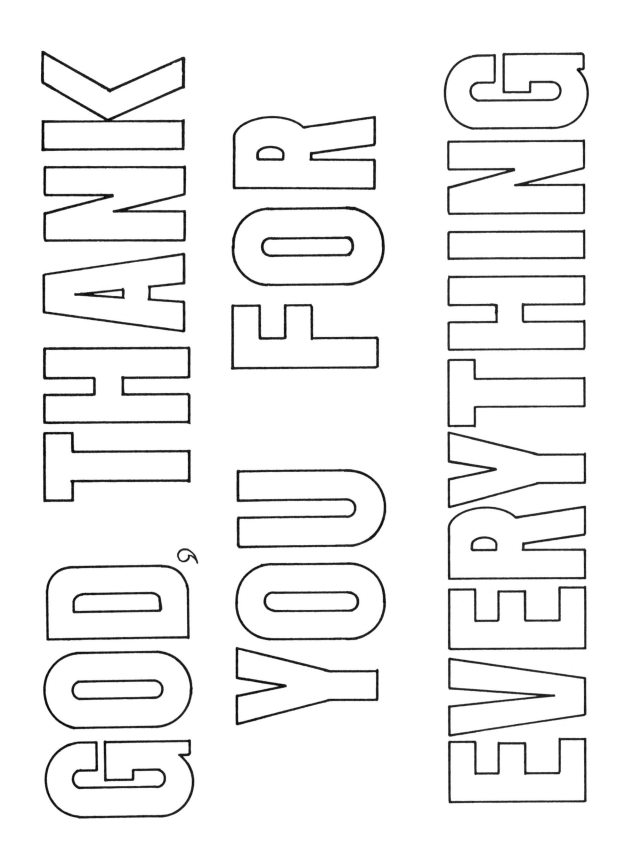

GOD, THANK YOU FOR EVERYTHING

SS897

CHRISTMAS PICTURE MATCH

"Today in the town of David a Savior has been born to you; he is Christ the Lord."
Luke 2:11

MATERIALS:

Poster board, letter-size envelopes, small Christmas pictures (see following page), 3" x 5" card.

SUGGESTED SETUP:

Cut off the flaps of several envelopes. Glue envelopes to the poster board for pockets. Make two copies of the small Christmas pictures and color them exactly alike. Put a different picture on each envelope.

Put a matching picture on separate 3" x 5" cards.

PROCEDURE:

- Lay the cards in front of the poster board.
- Let children take turns choosing a card, matching it to the corresponding picture and placing it in the pocket.

EXTENDED ACTIVITIES:

This activity can also be done with Easter stickers, Creation stickers, and Bible object stickers that can be found in Bible bookstores.

WHAT CHILDREN CAN LEARN FROM THIS EXPERIENCE:

- how to match items
- that God's Son, Jesus, was born on Christmas Day

NATIVITY DIORAMA

"They. . .found Mary and Joseph, and the baby, who was lying in the manger."

Luke 2:16

MATERIALS:

Pictures of Mary, Joseph, baby Jesus, animals, manger, star, hay (see following page), crayons, scissors, glue, shoe box, brown marking pens or paint.

SUGGESTED SETUP:

Make a copy of all the figures. If using paint, cover the table with newspaper.

PROCEDURE:

- Let children color the figures, and use marking pens or paint to cover the inside and outside of the shoe box and lid.
- Help children glue the figures to cardboard and cut them out.
- Place bottom of box on its side. Attach lid at an angle like a roof.
- Have the children place the figures inside the box to make a Nativity scene. Secure the figures in place with glue.
- Add the star to the edge of the stable roof.

WHAT CHILDREN CAN LEARN FROM THIS EXPERIENCE:

- how to paint
- how to make a diorama
- that Jesus was born in a stable on Christmas Day

Shining Star Publications, Copyright © 1991

SS897

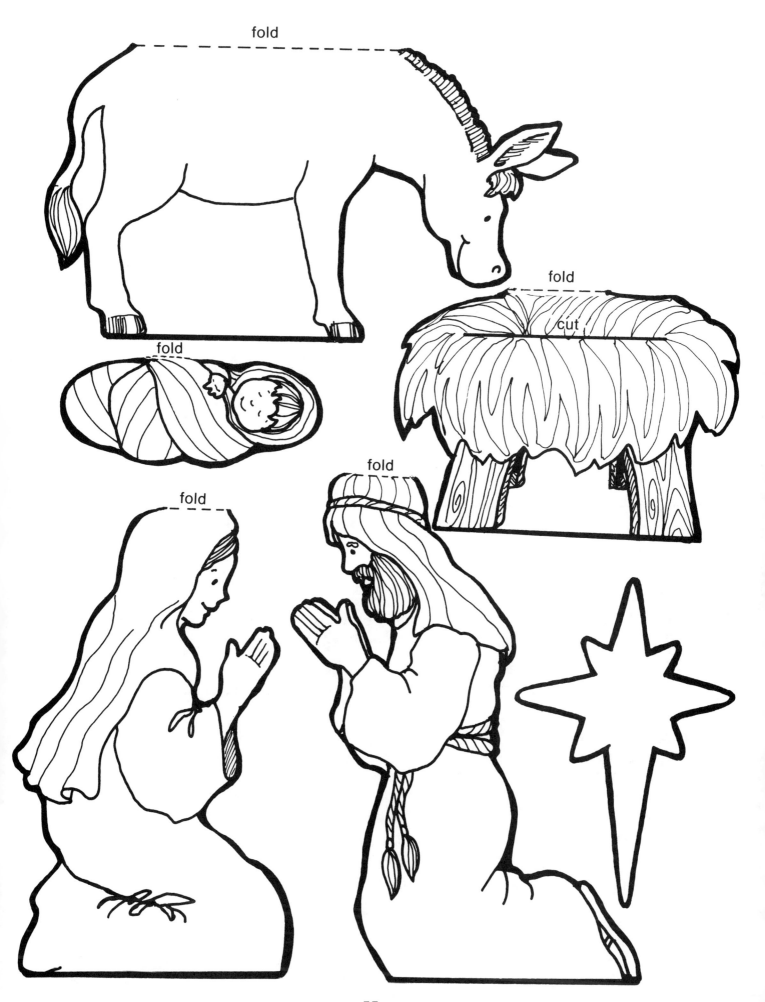

fold

fold

fold

cut

fold

fold

SS897

BUILD A NEIGHBORHOOD

"...Go into all the world and preach the good news to all creation."   Mark 16:15

MATERIALS:

Blocks, butcher or brown wrapping paper, crayons or marking pens, chenille wire, toy cars.

SUGGESTED SETUP:

Tape butcher or brown wrapping paper to the floor near the blocks.

PROCEDURE:

- Let children help you draw grass and roads on the paper.
- Have children build houses and a church on the grass with blocks.
- Show children how to make chenille-wire people to walk from house to house. They may pretend to be telling neighbors about Jesus and inviting them to church.
- Let children drive the toy cars on the roads. They may pretend to be going to church.

WHAT CHILDREN CAN LEARN FROM THIS EXPERIENCE:

- how to build with blocks
- that Jesus wants us to tell our friends and neighbors about Him and invite them to church

        SS897

WHERE CAN I PRAY?

"Do not be anxious about anything, but in everything, by prayer and petition, with thanksgiving, present your requests to God."   Philippians 4:6

MATERIALS:

Construction paper, pictures and house pattern (see following pages), scissors, glue, crayons or marking pens.

SUGGESTED SETUP:

You might want to make just one of these for the classroom, or have each child make one, or you may wish to do both. For classroom: enlarge the house pattern and pictures. For individual: have ready construction paper and copies of pictures for each child.

PROCEDURE:

For classroom:
- Use the enlarged house pattern to draw a house on a large sheet of construction paper.
- Cut open the door and windows on three sides.
- Place the house pattern against the background paper on the display area and mark where the windows and doors are.
- Color and cut out the enlarged pictures and glue on the background within the markings for the windows and doors. Tack or glue house pattern over the top of the pictures (making sure the pictures show through the windows and door).
- Open the windows and doors by folding back on the uncut side.

For individual houses:
- Give each child two sheets of construction paper (one for the house and one for the background).
- Help the children to repeat the procedures used for the classroom activity above.

EXTENDED ACTIVITIES:

For the classroom display or individual houses, the children might draw or find magazine pictures of other places where they can pray, such as in the car, at the playground, at school, at church, at a friend's house, at the doctor's office, etc. Glue the pictures onto the back of the house picture.

WHAT CHILDREN CAN LEARN FROM THIS EXPERIENCE:

- how to trace and cut
- that we can talk to God anywhere

SS897

SS897

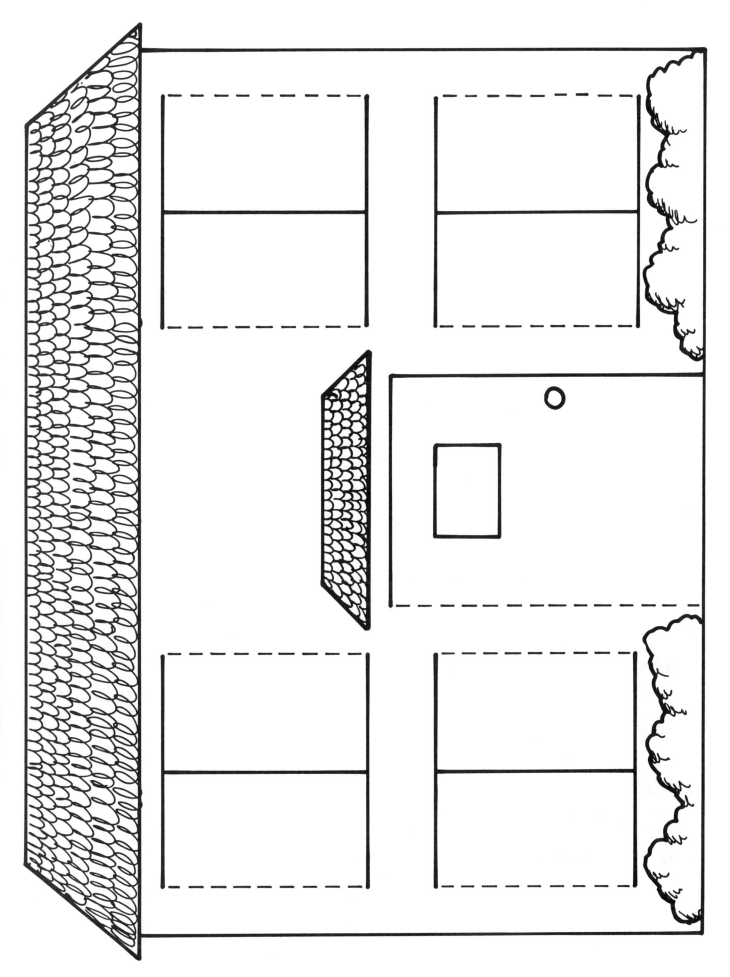

PRAISE INSTRUMENTS

"Sing to the Lord a new song; sing to the Lord, all the earth."   Psalm 96:1

MATERIALS:

Pattern instructions for making instruments (see following pages), cassette player and tape with praise music (optional).

SUGGESTED SETUP:

• Give each child materials to make at least one instrument.

PROCEDURE:

• Have each child make an instrument.
• Use the instruments to play praise music with the piano, cassette tape, or singing.

WHAT CHILDREN CAN LEARN FROM THIS EXPERIENCE:

• how to make different sounds with materials
• that we praise God with singing and musical instruments

SS897

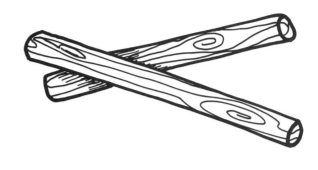

DRUM:

Use an oatmeal box. Glue on lid and wrapping paper, Con-Tact paper, or wallpaper to decorate.

RHYTHM STICKS:

Use ½" dowel sticks cut to 8" lengths. Sand and shellac the sticks.

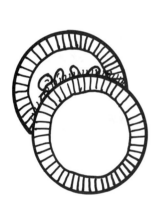

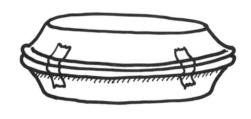

TAMBOURINE:

Use two foil pie pans or two paper plates. Put dried beans, small stones, or buttons in one of the pans or plates. Glue or tape the other plate over them. Decorate the paper plates with crayons.

FLUTE:

Roll a piece of 5" x 8" poster board lengthwise to make a tube. Tape the tube to close. Punch a hole in the flute as shown. Cover one end with waxed paper and secure it with a rubber band. Decorate.

SHAKER:

Use two strainers. Put beans, stones or buttons in one and cover with the other one. Tie handles together.

SANDPAPER BLOCKS:

Use two pieces of wood, 4″ x 5″. Tack coarse sandpaper to one side of the block. Put a knob on the other side and cover all sides but the sandpaper with shellac.

TRIANGLE:

Use a round curtain rod bent into a triangle as shown in the illustration. Use another piece of curtain rod or a spoon for the striker. Make a handle from a piece of cord tied to the top of the triangle.

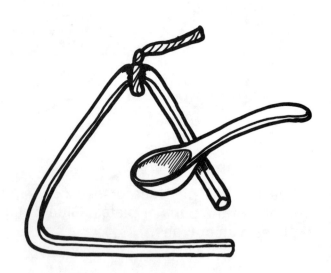

JINGLERS:

Use a Styrofoam cup. Put a hole on each side of the cup lip. String two or three bells on a length of yarn. Tie yarn to cup.

SS897

DRESS UP RELAY

"Blessed are the people whose God is the Lord."   Psalm 144:15b

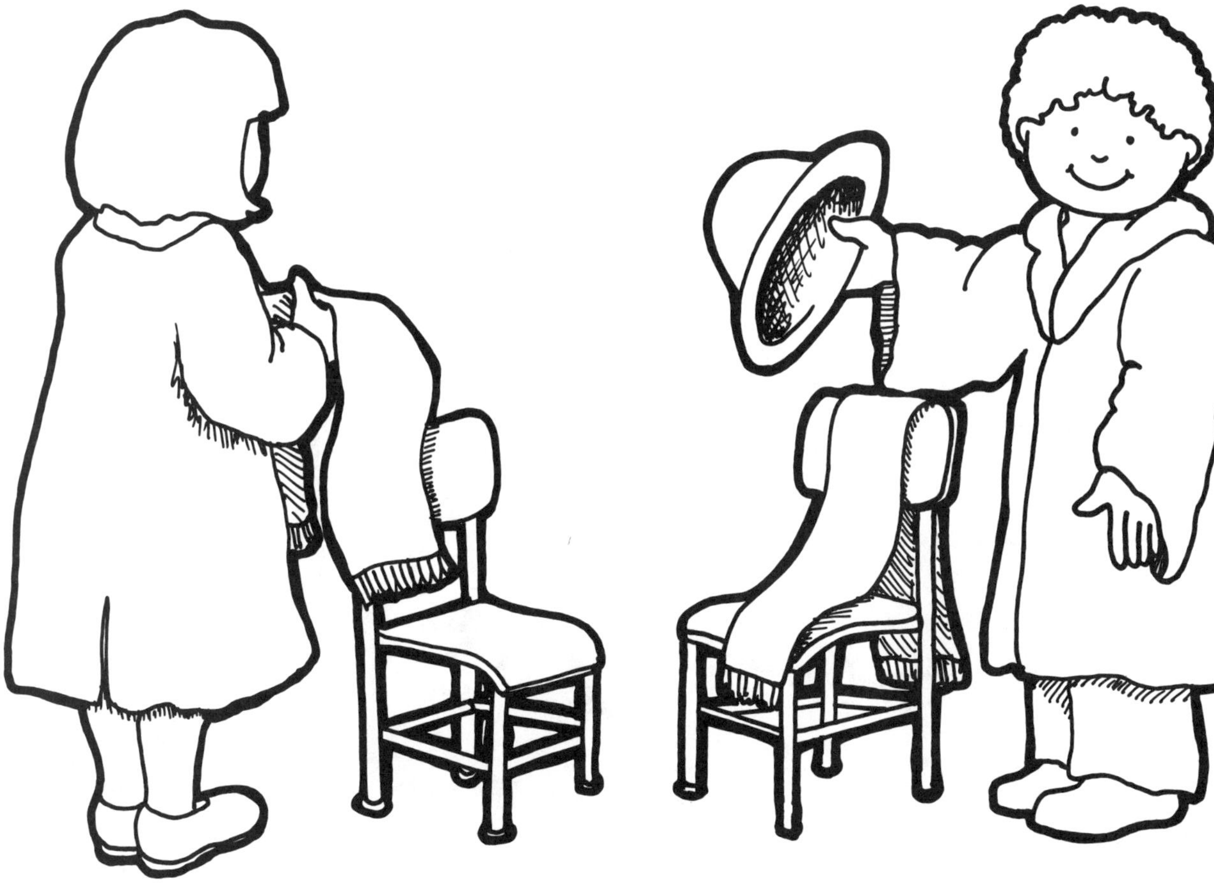

MATERIALS:

Dress up clothes such as hats, coats, aprons, and shoes for two teams (the clothing should be as much alike as possible so that one coat is not more difficult to put on than the other).

SUGGESTED SETUP:

- Place each set of clothing on individual chairs a few feet apart.

PROCEDURE:

- Divide the children into two teams and have them line up in front of the chairs with the clothing.
- When you say "go," the first person on each team puts on the clothing, takes it off, and hands it the next person on the team.
- The team that finishes first wins.

WHAT CHILDREN CAN LEARN FROM THIS EXPERIENCE:

- how to cooperate in a team effort
- that God wants us to work together

PUPPETS, PUPPETS, AND MORE PUPPETS

"And this gospel of the kingdom will be preached in the whole world. . . ."

Matthew 24:14a

MATERIALS:

Pattern page instructions (see following pages) for making a variety of puppets.

SUGGESTED SETUP:

Give children materials to make one or more puppets.

PROCEDURE:

- Let children choose which puppet or puppets they would like to make.
- Use the puppets to act out various situations, such as sharing, helping, being kind, telling others about Jesus, inviting someone to Sunday school, talking about feelings.
- Use the Bible puppets to act out Bible stories.

WHAT CHILDREN CAN LEARN FROM THIS EXPERIENCE:

- how to use a variety of materials
- how to act out situations
- practice telling others about Jesus

SS897

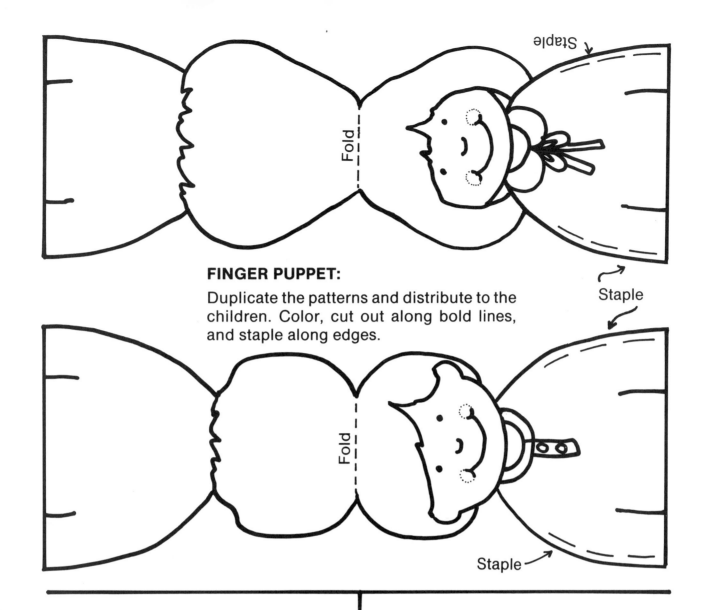

FINGER PUPPET:

Duplicate the patterns and distribute to the children. Color, cut out along bold lines, and staple along edges.

CEREAL BOX PUPPET:

Cut cereal box in half—leave one side uncut. Fold over. Draw face of person or animal on construction paper. Cut along mouth line. Glue to box.

GLOVE PUPPETS:

Cut fingers of glove 1½" from end. Draw on faces with marking pens. Use yarn for hair.

SS897

SPOON PUPPET:

Draw face and hair on round side of spoon. Use scraps of material for clothes.

THUMB PUPPET:

Draw face on thumb with marker. Use handkerchief or scrap of material for Bible costume.

PAPER CUP PUPPET:

Use paper cups. Poke pipe cleaners through sides. Draw features on Styrofoam ball with marking pens. Glue ball to cup bottom. Use yarn for hair. Put small stick or pipe cleaner into bottom of head and cup.

FIST PUPPET:

Draw face on hand. To talk—make a fist and move thumb up and down. To make a wig, stitch down the center of yarn strands and tape to hand.

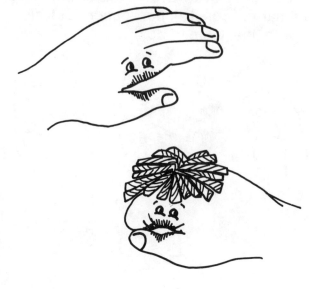

SS897

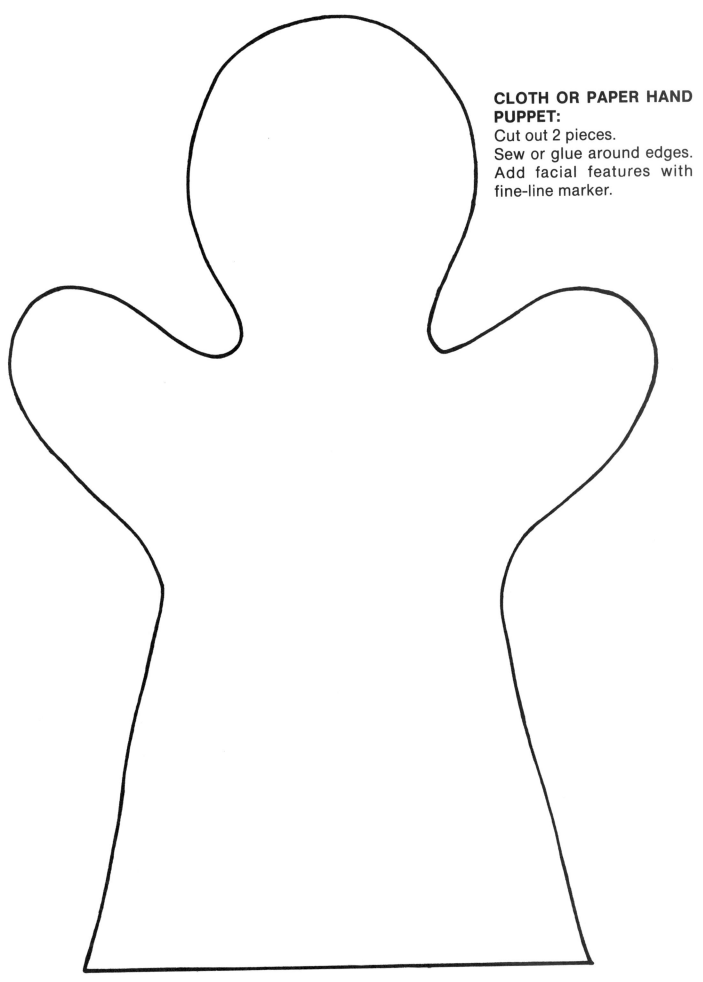

CLOTH OR PAPER HAND PUPPET:
Cut out 2 pieces.
Sew or glue around edges.
Add facial features with fine-line marker.

67

SS897

THE BIBLE TELLS ME SO!

"Heaven and earth will pass away, but my words will never pass away."   Luke 21:33

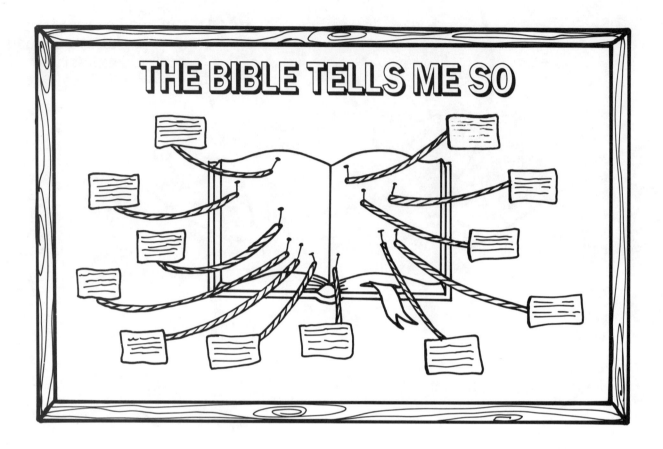

MATERIALS:

Bible pattern and display title (see following pages), bulletin board or display area, construction paper, scissors, crayons or marking pens, stapler, Bible verses the children are learning, yarn or ribbon.

SUGGESTED SETUP:

Cover the bulletin board or display area with paper. Enlarge Bible pattern and choose verses that will be displayed.

PROCEDURE:

- Let children cut out the Bible and staple to the display area.
- Let children color the title and staple to the display area.
- Help the children print Bible verses on squares of colored construction paper.
- Staple Bible verses around the Bible.
- Attach ribbon or yarn from the Bible to the verses.

WHAT CHILDREN CAN LEARN FROM THIS EXPERIENCE:

- practice in printing
- that the verses they are learning come from God's word, the Bible

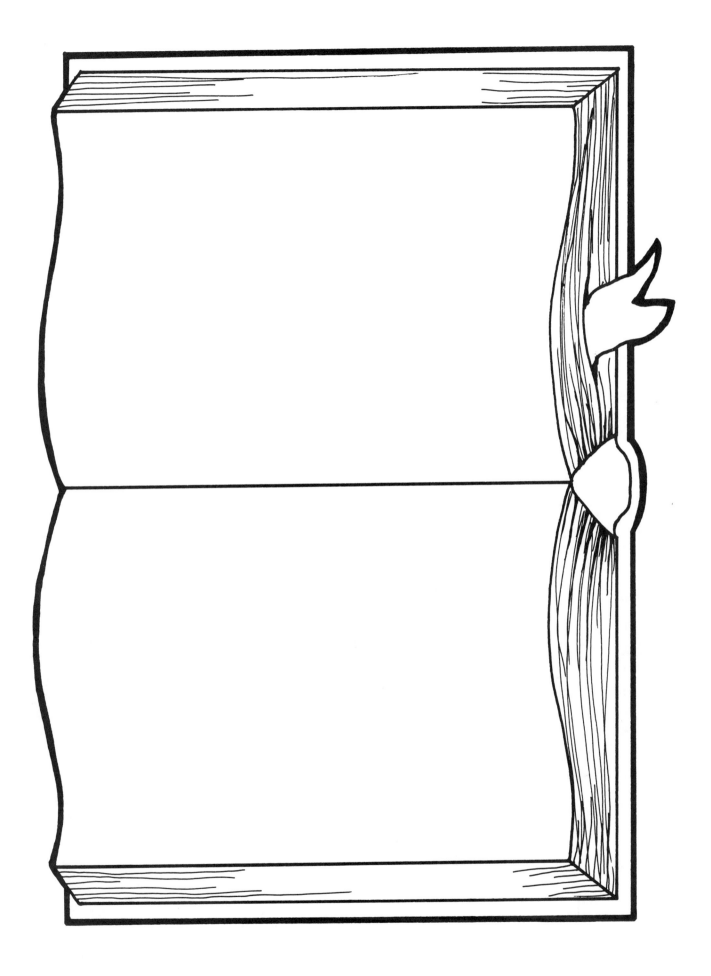

SS897

THE BIBLE TELLS ME SO

70

I CAN!

"I can do everything through him who gives me strength."   Philippians 4:13

MATERIALS:

Three poster boards, three plastic lids, construction paper, paper fasteners, marking pen, pictures (see following pages), glue, scissors.

SUGGESTED SETUP:

Make a copy of the pictures and lay out all the materials. Plan to do one board at a time or divide the children into three groups and have each group work on one board.

PROCEDURE:

- Help the children print the words *I can share, I can be kind, I can help* at the top of the boards as the titles.
- Have the children color and cut out the pictures for each board.
- Help the children make a spinner for each board with the plastic lids. Cut three arrows from construction paper and attach one to each lid with a paper fastener.
- Attach a spinner to the middle of each board with the paper fastener.
- Hang the boards on a bulletin board, wall, back of piano or sides of a large box.
- Have children turn the spinner and tell how they can share items shown, be kind or help in situations shown.

EXTENDED ACTIVITY:

Children might also turn the spinner and act out the situations shown.

WHAT CHILDREN CAN LEARN FROM THIS EXPERIENCE:

- that we can share, be kind, and help in many situations
- that Jesus will help us to share, be kind, and help because that is the way He wants us to live

     SS897

SHARE

SS897

KIND

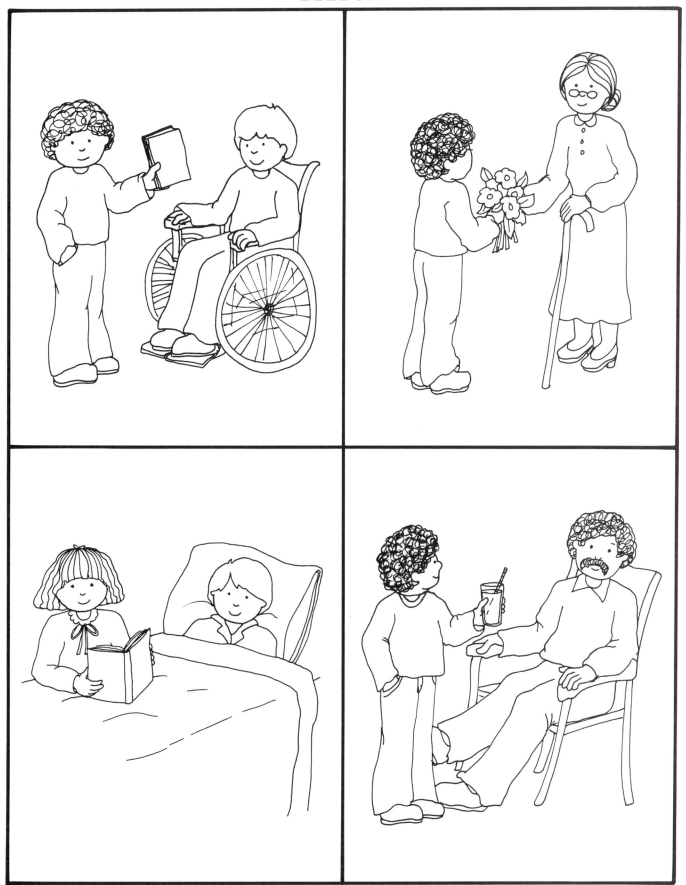

73

HELP

SS897

EASTER TREE

"But Christ has indeed been raised from the dead. . . ."   I Corinthians 15:20a

MATERIALS:

Bare tree branch, bucket filled with sand, plastic eggs, egg dye, yarn or string, craft needle, Easter symbols (see following page); if you don't use plastic eggs: paper egg shapes (see following page), crayons, glue.

SUGGESTED SETUP:

Make a copy of the Easter symbols and have one plastic egg or paper egg shape for each child.

PROCEDURE:

- If using plastic eggs, bore a small hole in each end of the egg with a pin or large needle.
- If using paper eggs, trace egg pattern on white construction paper, color and cut out.
- Glue the symbols on the eggs—one to each egg.
- Put the branch in the bucket.
- Help children attach the yarn or string by threading it through a craft needle and tying a knot at the end. Pull the needle through the egg.
- Hang the eggs from the branch.

WHAT CHILDREN CAN LEARN FROM THIS EXPERIENCE:

- the different symbols that represent Easter
- that Jesus came alive again on Easter

     SS897

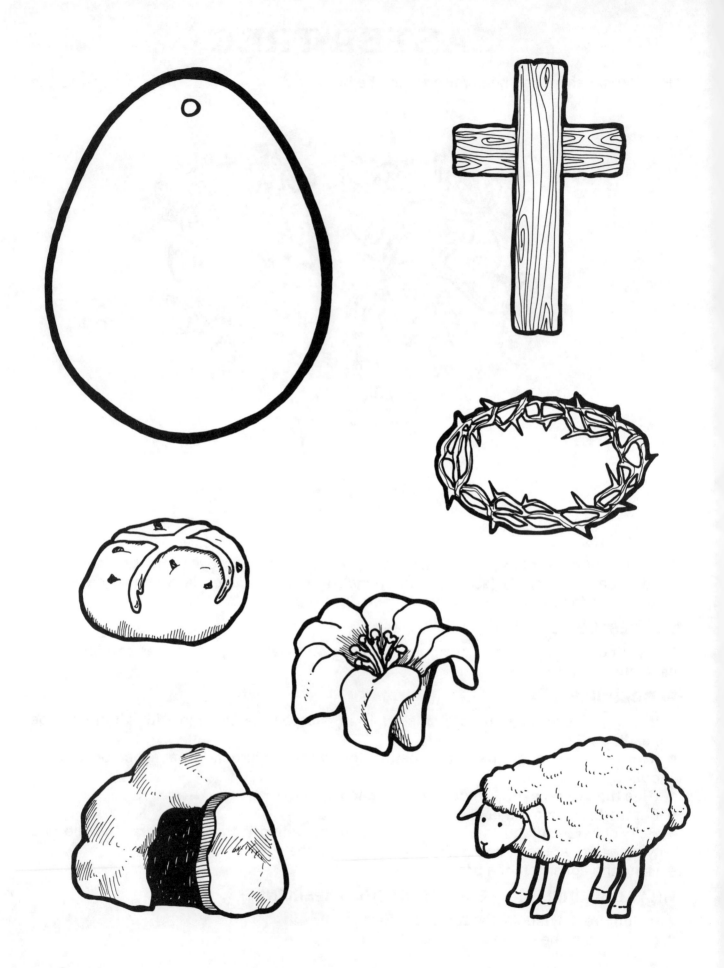

SS897

WRITING PRAISE SONGS

"Sing to him a new song; play skillfully, and shout for joy."   Psalm 33:3

MATERIALS:

Song sheet (see following page), poster board, stapler, marking pen, cassette player and blank tape, rhythm instruments.

SUGGESTED SETUP:

Enlarge the song sheet, staple to the poster board and hang on the bulletin board or wall. Or, print the words of the songs on the poster board.

PROCEDURE:

- Help children think of a last line for the songs.
- Sing the songs and play rhythm instruments.
- Help children write a whole song and sing it, too.
- Record the children singing and playing instruments on the cassette tape and let them hear it.

WHAT CHILDREN CAN LEARN FROM THIS EXPERIENCE:

- how to write songs of praise
- that singing is one way to praise God and Jesus

                    SS897

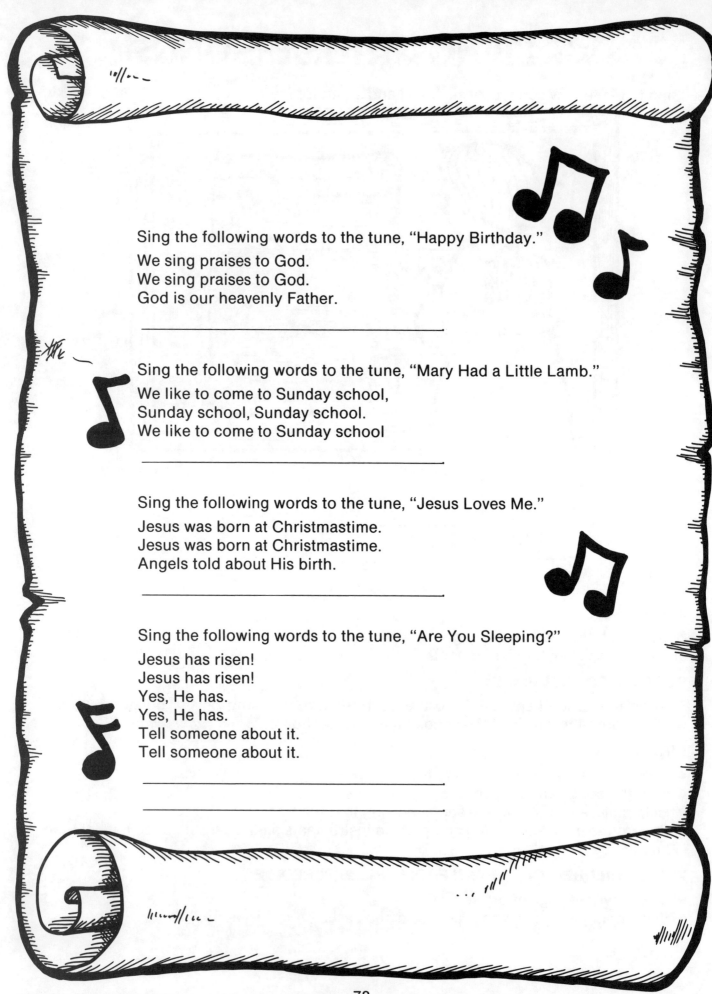

Sing the following words to the tune, "Happy Birthday."

We sing praises to God.
We sing praises to God.
God is our heavenly Father.

_____

Sing the following words to the tune, "Mary Had a Little Lamb."

We like to come to Sunday school,
Sunday school, Sunday school.
We like to come to Sunday school

_____

Sing the following words to the tune, "Jesus Loves Me."

Jesus was born at Christmastime.
Jesus was born at Christmastime.
Angels told about His birth.

_____

Sing the following words to the tune, "Are You Sleeping?"

Jesus has risen!
Jesus has risen!
Yes, He has.
Yes, He has.
Tell someone about it.
Tell someone about it.

_____

_____

Shining Star Publications, Copyright © 1991 SS897

REACH FOR THE STARS!

"Those who are wise will shine like the brightness of the heavens, and those who lead many to righteousness, like the stars for ever and ever."   Daniel 12:3

MATERIALS:

Construction paper, star and letter patterns (see following page), crayons or marking pens, stapler, bulletin board, wall space or other display area.

SUGGESTED SETUP:

Make a copy of the letters for the display title, and copies of the stars for patterns. Cover the bulletin board, wall space or other display area with blue paper.

PROCEDURE:

● Help the children trace their handprints on construction paper, one handprint for each child. Have them cut out the handprints and print their names on them.
● Help the children staple handprints in the lower part of the display area.
● Let the children trace the title letters; color, cut out, and staple them to the display.
● Let the children trace the star pattern on white construction paper and cut it out. They should do several stars.
● As children learn Bible verses, print the verse reference and their names on the stars and staple them to the top area of the display.

WHAT CHILDREN CAN LEARN FROM THIS EXPERIENCE:

● that God wants us to learn His Word

REACH FOR THE STARS

80

SS897

CORNUCOPIA THANKS!

"Now, our God, we give you thanks, and praise your glorious name." I Chronicles 29:13

MATERIALS:

Cornucopia, pictures, letters (see following pages), scissors, crayons, stapler, display area.

SUGGESTED SETUP:

Cover the display area with yellow or orange paper. Enlarge the cornucopia and duplicate the pictures and letters.

PROCEDURE:

- Help children cut out the cornucopia, color, and staple it to the display area.
- Let children color, cut out, and staple pictures to the display area; have pictures spilling out of the cornucopia.
- Let children color the letters, cut them out, and staple them on the display area above the cornucopia.

EXTENDED ACTIVITIES:

- Duplicate pictures of fruits and vegetables from this book (found on page 5), and add to the display.
- Find pictures of things in magazines that we are thankful for and add to the display.

WHAT CHILDREN CAN LEARN FROM THIS EXPERIENCE:

- how to say the new word *cornucopia*; that another name for cornucopia is *horn of plenty*
- to think about all the things we have and can thank God for

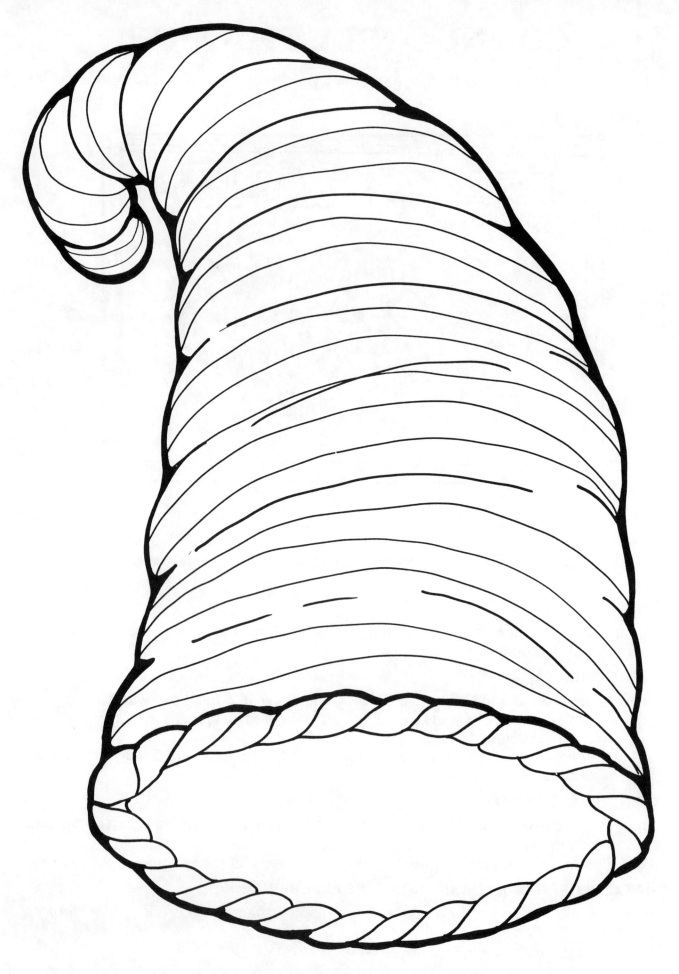

CORNUCOPIA THANKS!

SS897

WE HELP OUR MISSIONARIES

"Whoever serves me must follow me; and where I am, my servant also will be. My Father will honor the one who serves me."

John 12:26

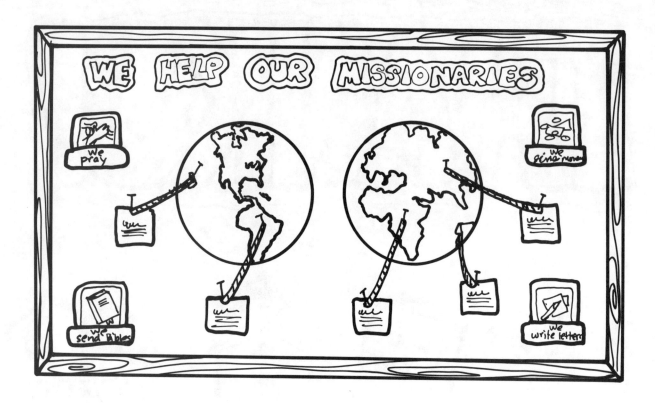

MATERIALS:

Globe, pictures, letters (see following pages), scissors, crayons, stapler, yarn, display area and covering, pictures of missionaries.

SUGGESTED SETUP:

Enlarge the picture of the globe. Cover the display area with blue paper. Make copies of pictures and letters.

PROCEDURE:

- Help children color the globe and place on the display area in two pieces.
- Let children color the title letters, cut them out, and staple them to the display area.
- Let children color the pictures, cut them out, and staple them on each side of and beneath the globe.
- Add pictures of missionaries to the display. Attach yarn from the missionaries' pictures to the places where they serve.

WHAT THE CHILDREN CAN LEARN FROM THIS EXPERIENCE:

- what we can do for missionaries
- places in the world where missionaries serve

WE HELP OUR MISSIONARIES

We pray.

We give money.

We send Bibles.

We write letters.

SS897

Western world

Eastern world

86

SS897

GOD IS WITH ME EVERYWHERE!

"Trust in the Lord forever, for the Lord, the Lord, is the Rock eternal."   Isaiah 26:4

MATERIALS:

Map of the United States, transportation pictures, pictures of vacation places, letters (see following pages), bulletin board or wall space for display area, crayons, scissors, stapler, yarn, tape.

SUGGESTED SETUP:

Enlarge picture of map for the display area. Make copies of the transportation and vacation pictures and letters.

PROCEDURE:

● Let children color and cut out the vacation pictures and letters.
● Help children staple or tape the pictures around the map and pin a length of yarn from the pictures to various places on the map.
● Help children staple or tape the letters at the top of the display for a title.
● Have children choose one of the transportation pictures, color it, and cut it out.
● Then, have children place their transportation pictures near places they know they will go on vacation, where they have gone, or where they would like to go. The children might do this each week during the summer.

WHAT CHILDREN CAN LEARN FROM THIS EXPERIENCE:

● the different places people go on their vacations
● that God is always with us wherever we go

                    SS897

ZOO

Train Station

SS897

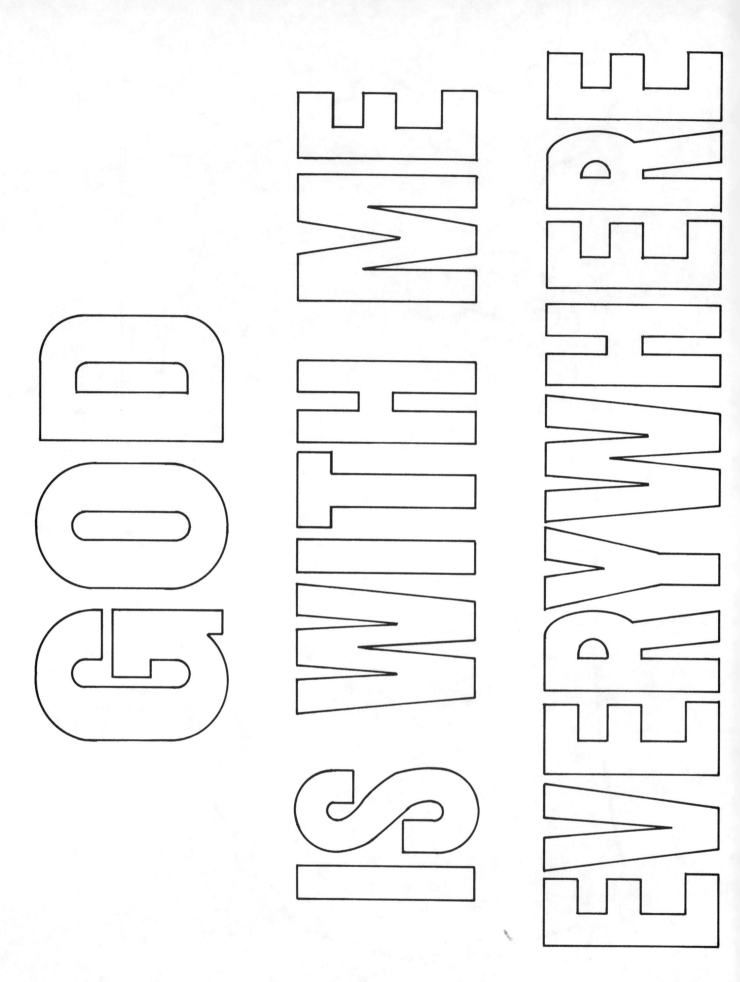

GOD IS WITH ME EVERYWHERE

90

CHURCH HELPERS

"Dear friends, since God so loved us, we also ought to love one another."   I John 4:11

MATERIALS:

Church pattern (from page 45), people face patterns and letters (see following pages), scissors, crayons, stapler or tape, bulletin board or wall space for display, small squares of construction paper for labels.

SUGGESTED SETUP:

Enlarge church pattern and staple or tape it to the display area. Make copies of the face patterns and letters.

PROCEDURE:

- Let children color and cut out the title letters and staple or tape them to the top of the display.
- Talk about the people who are church helpers, such as: teachers, pastor, choir director, ushers, custodians, organist/pianist, etc. Let children complete face patterns for each of these people and staple or tape them to the display area around the church. Use the construction paper squares to label each person's picture with his job title.
- Lead children to realize that they are church helpers, too, when they help give out papers, pick up toys, etc. Have them complete a face pattern of themselves for the display.

EXTENDED ACTIVITY:

- Ask one or more church helpers to come and talk to the children and tell what they do at church, why they do it, and what abilities they have which allows them to be a church helper.

WHAT CHILDREN CAN LEARN FROM THIS EXPERIENCE:

- that the church has a lot of different kinds of helpers
- that God wants everyone to be a church helper

SS897

SS897

Church helpers can be personalized with glasses, hair color or style change, etc.

SS897

THE BEST GIFT—YOU!

"Share with God's people who are in need."   Romans 12:13a

MATERIALS:

Child pattern, letters (see following pages), a small box for each child, Christmas wrapping paper, stapler, tacks or tape, scissors, crayons, gift tags, bulletin board or wall space for display. Or, construction paper and instant camera and film.

SUGGESTED SETUP:

Cover the display area with white paper. Make copies of the child pattern and letters for title.

PROCEDURE:

- Help the children wrap boxes in Christmas paper—one for each child.
- Have children color and cut out child figures to represent themselves.
- Have children color and cut out the letters and staple or tape to the top of the display area.
- Help children staple, tape, or tack their boxes on the display area.
- Help children put their figures in the boxes so that the top of the figure sticks above the edge of the box.
- Help children print the words *To God, With Love* and their names on gift tags and tape them on the fronts of the boxes.

OPTIONAL:

Use an instant camera to take a picture of each child. Have children glue pictures to construction paper and print *To God, With Love* and their names under their pictures. Staple or tape the pictures around one Christmas-wrapped box with a paper figure of a child in it that has been stapled or tacked to the middle of the display area.

WHAT CHILDREN CAN LEARN FROM THIS EXPERIENCE:

- how to wrap presents
- that the best gift we can give God is ourselves

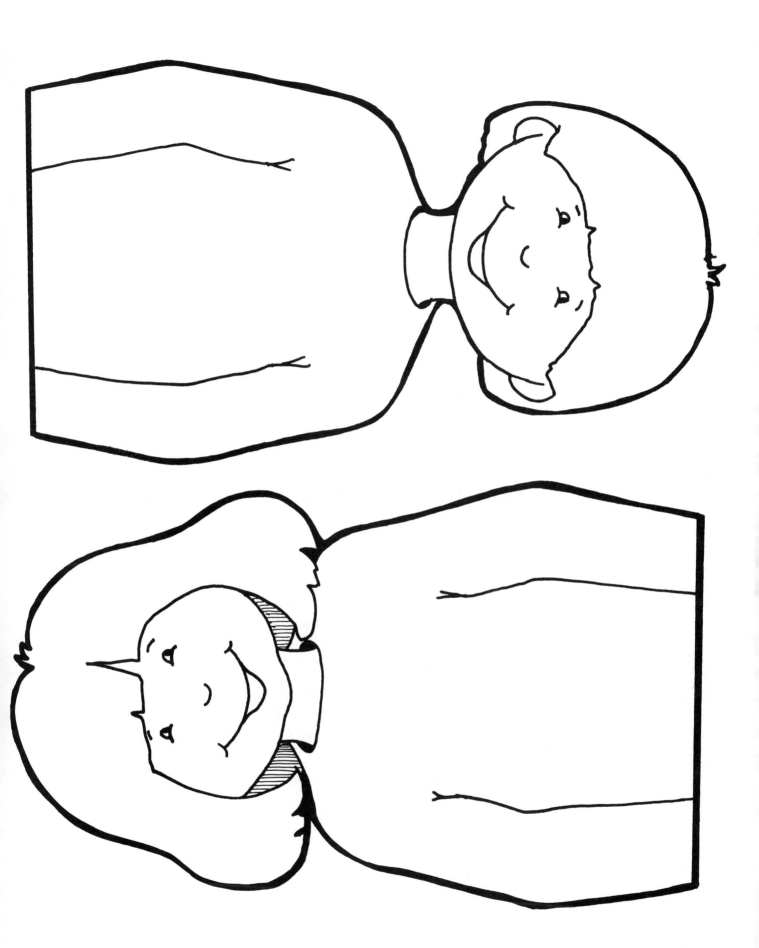

 SS897

THE BEST GIFT- YOU !